Looking at Animal Parts

Let's Look at Animal Feathers

by Wendy Perkins

Consulting Editor: Gail Saunders-Smith, PhD

Consultant: Suzanne B. McLaren, Collections Manager
Section of Mammals, Carnegie Museum of Natural History
Edward O'Neil Research Center, Pittsburgh, Pennsylvania

Capstone
press

Mankato, Minnesota

Pebble Plus is published by Capstone Press,
151 Good Counsel Drive, P.O. Box 669, Mankato, Minnesota 56002.
www.capstonepress.com

1 2 3 4 5 6 11 10 09 08 07 06

Library of Congress Cataloging-in-Publication Data
Perkins, Wendy, 1957–
     Let's look at animal feathers / by Wendy Perkins.
     p. cm.—(Pebble plus. Looking at animal parts)
     Summary: "Simple text and photographs present animal feathers, how they work, and how different
animals use them"—Provided by publisher.
     Includes bibliographical references and index.
     ISBN-13: 978-0-7368-6350-6 (hardcover)
     ISBN-10: 0-7368-6350-8 (hardcover)
     1. Feathers—Juvenile literature. I. Title. II. Series.
QL697.P47 2007
598.147—dc22   2006000998

Editorial Credits
Sarah L. Schuette, editor; Kia Adams, set designer; Renée Doyle, cover production; Kelly Garvin, photo
     researcher/photo editor

Photo Credits
Digital Vision, cover
James P. Rowan, 14–15
Lynn M. Stone, 5
McDonald Wildlife Photography/Joe McDonald, 10–11, 12–13
Minden Pictures/Konrad Wothe, 18–19; Norbert Wu, 6–7
Nature Picture Library/Martha Holmes, 8–9
Pete Carmichael, 20–21
Shutterstock/Philip Erche, 1; Sandra May Caldwell, 17

Note to Parents and Teachers

The Looking at Animal Parts set supports national science standards related to
life science. This book describes and illustrates animal feathers. The images support
early readers in understanding the text. The repetition of words and phrases helps early
readers learn new words. This book also introduces early readers to subject-specific
vocabulary words, which are defined in the Glossary section. Early readers may need
assistance to read some words and to use the Table of Contents, Glossary, Read More,
Internet Sites, and Index sections of the book.

Table of Contents

Feathers at Work

Feathers help birds fly
and keep warm.
Birds use their feathers
to hide and show off.

A penguin chick's
soft down feathers puff up
in the cold.
The chick stays warm
and dry.

The chick grows up.

New waterproof feathers form.

Now, the penguin can swim.

Kinds of Feathers

Eagles have long, stiff feathers for flying.
Layers of feathers keep eagles warm and dry in the air.

Flamingos have pink feathers.

The color comes

from the food flamingos eat.

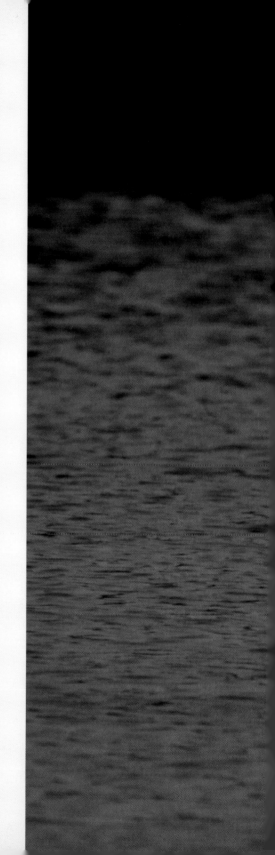

Peacocks fan out
their huge tail feathers.
Peacocks strut around
to attract females.

Cockatoos have crests of feathers on their heads. The feathers stand straight up to scare predators away.

Female mallards have
feathers that help them hide.
The feathers blend in
with plants on the shore.

Awesome Feathers

Flashy or fluffy,

birds use their feathers

to fly, hide, and show off.

Glossary

attract—to get the attention of another animal

crest—a row of feathers on a bird's head

down—the soft feathers of a bird; young penguins, chickens, and other birds have down before their adult feathers grow.

predator—an animal that hunts another animal for food

strut—to walk proudly in order to show off

waterproof—able to keep water out

Read More

Mayer, Cassie. *Feathers.* Body Coverings. Chicago: Heinemann Library, 2006.

Taylor, Barbara. *Birds and Other Flying Animals.* Animal Close-Ups. Columbus, Ohio: Peter Bedrick Books, 2003.

Twist, Clint. *Feathery Creatures.* Animal Touch. Columbus, Ohio: Waterbird Books, 2005.

Internet Sites

FactHound offers a safe, fun way to find Internet sites related to this book. All of the sites on FactHound have been researched by our staff.

Here's how:

1. Visit *www.facthound.com*

2. Choose your grade level.

3. Type in this book ID **0736863508** for age-appropriate sites. You may also browse subjects by clicking on letters, or by clicking on pictures and words.

4. Click on the **Fetch It** button.

FactHound will fetch the best sites for you!

Index

cockatoos, 16

color, 12, 18

crests, 16

down, 6

eagles, 10

females, 14, 18

flamingos, 12

layers, 10

mallards, 18

peacocks, 14

penguins, 6, 8

predators, 16

warm, 4, 6, 10

waterproof, 8

Word Count: 136
Grade: 1
Early-Intervention Level: 14